Hope
through
Heartsongs

Other books written and illustrated by
Mattie J.T. Stepanek

Heartsongs

Journey Through Heartsongs

Hope through Heartsongs

Written and Illustrated

by

Mattie J.T. Stepanek

Poet & Peacemaker

HYPERION

NEW YORK

ISBN: 0-7868-6944-5

Hyperion books are available for special promotions and premiums.
For details contact Hyperion Special Markets, 77 West 66th Street, 11th floor,
New York, New York, 10023, or call 212-456-0100.

10 9 8 7 6 5 4 3 2 1

This book is dedicated to *all* people
who are struggling to find hope...
especially the children of our world and their families.
Remember to play after every storm!

—Love, Mattie

Acknowledgments

Thank you to VSP Books for first making me a published "poet and peacemaker," and to Hyperion for helping me spread the message of my heartsongs in a huge way.

Thank you to the Muscular Dystrophy Association, Children's National Medical Center, and Children's Hospice International for giving me the chance to live, and to love life while I am living it.

Thank you to Oprah Winfrey and Jimmy Carter for giving me hope, and for teaching kids and other people that they can be real friends with real-life heroes.

Thank you to Jerry Lewis, Ed McMahon, Chris Cuomo, Laura Bush, Gary Zukav, Bernie Siegel, Harold Schaitberger, Mia Hamm, and Mike Myers for letting me talk with the "famous people" and learn that they are seeking hope just like everyone else.

Thank you to Sandy, Lyn, Mike, Valerie, Mollie, Teresa, Candie, Leslie, D.J., Tom, Brian, Libby, Shelly, Kelly, "J.K.," Amy, the Firefighters, the Harley folks, the D'Anna family, Dr. Kim, Dr. Fink, Laura, Rita, Regina, Peggy, Terry, Marissa, Cynda, Bob, Mary Ellen, Bob, Deneen, Patricia, Judy, all of my teachers, and most of all, my mom, for protecting and supporting me, and for helping me trust in grown-ups to hear and meet the needs of children.

Thank you to Nick, Ben, Hope, and Marie, and to Hedder, Jamie-D., Chris, Arlo, Kunpal, Jessie, Kenny, Jimmy, Tommy, Amanda, Heather, David, Daniel, Ryan, Erin, Neil, Sarah, Will, Alex, Kristen, and Guder for letting me grow and be with some of the best kin and friends in the world.

Love, Mattie

Foreword

In the past, most of us were born limited to the perceptions of the five senses. From this perspective, the entire universe consists of what we can see, smell, hear, taste, and touch. Each of us is a body and a mind, but no more. A relative few of us were born able to see beyond the five senses. From this perspective, each individual is much more than a body and a mind, and, in addition, is an immortal soul. For such individuals, the five senses do not disappear, but another sensory capability is active. That is the perception of the soul.

The perception of the soul is multisensory perception. Multisensory perception is now emerging in millions of humans. They see meaning in everyday circumstances. They yearn for meaning more than for security and comfort, and even more than wealth, fame, and success. They long for the needs of their souls—harmony, cooperation, sharing, and reverence for Life.

As multisensory perception emerges throughout the human family, the human experience appears as more than a journey from birth to death. It appears also as a chapter in a larger book with a multitude of chapters. Each chapter is a life in the Earth school—the learning environment of the five senses—and the book is the chronicle of a soul as it enters the Earth school again and again to learn and to contribute.

Chapters begin and end, but the book continues. Five-sensory humans mistake their lives for the book. A multisensory human sees his life as a chapter in the book. He sees the lives of others in the same way. A multisensory human does not think of herself as beginning with her birth or ending with her death any more than she thinks that a book ends when one of its chapters comes to conclusion. The unfolding history of the book becomes more and more visible in each chapter—in each life.

This is apparent when a young person sees, thinks, speaks, acts, and feels with wisdom that a few years in the Earth school cannot explain. Mattie Stepanek was eleven years old when I first spoke with him, yet he spoke to me of peace, humility, and gratitude. He spoke of giving gifts that would benefit others even after he died. He spoke of heavenly Angels and angels that are even more important to him—everyday Angels. You and I are everyday Angels when we are kind to each other, listen to each other, care about each other, and help each other. He also spoke of messages from his heart, which he called heartsongs. His desire was to be a peace-maker and, through his poetry, create peace and help others discover their heartsongs and listen to them.

When you desire the same things, you tap into the accumulating wisdom of the book in which you are a chapter. Then you become an inspiration to others in the same way that Mattie is an inspiration to us. We are each Angels-in-the-making, and that is why we can see and honor in others, such as Mattie, the goal that each of us is traveling toward. Mattie reminds us of that goal and makes us thankful.

—Gary Zukav

Introduction

Hello everybody. This is Matthew Joseph Thaddeus Stepanek, but I prefer to be called Mattie. Welcome to *Hope Through Heartsongs*, my third book to be published. The words that fill these pages are created and joined in the form of poetry. Therefore, it will be considered a work of fiction, like first my two books, *Heartsongs* and *Journey Through Heartsongs*. But I want to tell you this: the message of this book is not fiction…it is true.

My poetry comes from my heart and from my life. I have been creating poetry about my feelings, my happiness, my pain, my dreams, my fears, my insights, and more, since I was three years old. These passages speak about my experiences with disability, death, and divorce, and they speak about the possibilities of strength, future, and peace. Sometimes, a poem just comes to me, and I can't type fast enough to keep up with my thoughts. Sometimes, an idea comes to me that will become a poem, but I just capture a thought and write the poem later (sometimes months or even years later). And sometimes, a poem is a part of a school assignment, or is born from an essay or journal entry I have written at some time. But at all times, my poetry is a part of my heartsong, whether the reality of the message is sad or serious or silly or significant.

I first began using the term "heartsong" when I was about five years old. I was creating some poetry, and happened to be wearing a sweatshirt with a little music-maker inside the fabric. I leaned against something while I was making my poetry, and the music began. I whispered, "Mommy, listen, that's my heartsong." And I immediately wrote a poem, called "Heartsong," that told all about it. I call it my "master poem," and included it in my first books to help people understand.

A heartsong is something deep inside each of us. It's our sense of why we are here and how we can keep going. It is like a purpose. It may be to live as a mommy or a daddy, or a firefighter or a delivery person, or a child with a disability who teaches others about patience and love and acceptance. Heartsongs are usually easy to hear when we are young, but we sometimes get too busy or hurt or angry to listen to them as we get older. And just like any gift that isn't cared for or used well, it is possible to forget how to listen to the message of each song. But even if we completely lose our heartsong, we can share someone else's song until we are able to reawaken or recreate our own.

The message of the heartsongs that I am sharing in this book is hope. Hope is essential to our lives each day. With hope, we can optimistically anticipate our future, rather than merely awaiting it, or allowing it, to occur. Hope brings brightness to each point of view, and a confident desire to be proactive and enthusiastic in meeting challenges and in overcoming obstacles. It is important to know, however, that to have hope, we must also explore the feelings and realities that come with our struggles—personal struggles, struggles with other people, and struggles with events that take place around our world.

It would be easy for each of us to stay shocked, angry, hurt, or sad with all the difficult things that we face in life. And even though it is difficult and sometimes almost overwhelming to examine feelings related to loss and loneliness and alarming turmoil, it is the only way that we can grow, individually and together. We cannot let sad or traumatic events, or even acts of terror, be the death of hope. That is why this book explores these issues, and finds that in spite of each struggle, we can and will find hope if we choose to do so.

If I could offer each person a wish for being, it would be a spirit of understanding and faith. If I could offer all people a wish for being with each other, it would be a spirit of acceptance and forgiveness. And if I could offer our world a wish, it would be a spirit of peace, so that we can *be*, together. My prayer now is that by sharing my heartsongs, their message may offer a spirit of hope, which may inspire the courage needed for people to make the choice and accept the offers of all of these wishes. Thank you for sharing my heartsongs with me, and with others.

Love,
Mattie

Contents

Hope
for
Within

Choice Lesson

Growth brings change.
Unpredictable change,
Which can bring
Hesitancy to optimism.
It is essential that we cope
With the realities of the past
And the uncertainties of the future
With a pure and chosen hope.
Not a blind faith,
But a strengthened choice.
Then, we can have the
Fortitude and wisdom necessary
To integrate life's many lessons
That collect beyond points in time.
Growing like this will help
Build a good future,
For individuals,
For communities,
And for the world.

February 2000

Birth-Tears

When I was a little
Teeny-tiny baby
And I came out of
My mommy's womb,
I cried.
That's what most babies
Do when they are born.
Do you know why
I cried when I was born?
I cried for the same
Reason that most babies
Cry when they are born.
I cried because I was so happy.
I cried because I got to come
And live in this family.
I cried because God was
So good to let me have
The best mommy in the world.
And that is why most
Babies cry when they are born...
They are happy birth-tears
Because we are so happy
To be in the best families.

June 1996

About Normal

Right now,
I don't know what Normal is
Anymore.
That's because Normal has been changing
So much,
So often,
Lately.
For a long while of lately.
I'd like Normal to be
Okayness.
Good health...
Emotional health,
Medical health,
Spiritual health.
I'd like Normal to be
Like that.
I'd like Normal to stay,
Like that.
For now though,
I know that Normal won't be normal
For a little while...
But somehow,
Sometime,
Even if things are not Normal,
They'll be okay.
That's because I believe
In the great scheme of things,
And Life.

May 2001

It Happened Anyway

When Jamie died,
And I didn't even understand
The eternity of my sadness,
I wished I could have prevented it.
But then, I remember,
It happened anyway.
When I rest in my bed,
And dream about how I could have
Lived and played with my brother,
I wish I could have stopped his death.
But then, I remember,
It happened anyway.
When I look at pictures,
And imagine what he would be like
Now a dozen years old,
I wish I could have saved him from agelessness.
But then, I remember,
It happened anyway.
When I hug our mommy,
And we think of why, and how, and
When he was with us and left us,
We wish we could have prevented it,
And stopped his death, and saved him from
Never needing breath for birthday candles...
But then, we remember, though we don't understand,
It happened anyway.

November 2001

6

Dear God,

I've been having these dreams,
That make me think that it is real,
And that it will really happen.
Like about a monster taking me away from
Home without anything to take with me and
I never see my mother again.
Dear God,
Please help me have some special medicine
That will get rid of all these nightmares
About going away, and leaving, and dying.
Dear God,
I will thank You for the special medicine,
Even if it's invisible medicine that is
Inside of all the healthy food I eat everyday,
Or inside of all the meditation I do everyday.
Dear God,
I send You big hugs and big kisses, and
You will send me the invisible medicine
To cure this scariness and
To get over these feelings and nightmares.
Please put it into all of the food that I eat
So they won't come ever again,
Even while I am still getting better.
I need to get rid of this tiredness in my heart.
Amen.

August 1996

Land of Loneliness

Sometimes,
I feel like I have
Broken through
The wall into the
Land of Loneliness.
I cry in my mind, and
I cry in my heart, but
I never cry in my eyes.
I don't want anyone
To know how
Sad and how
Lonely and how
Different I feel.
I know that I don't
Always feel this way,
But I feel this way now.
I don't like feeling this
Way now, or any-ever.

April 1996

Shared Tears

Sometimes,
I get sad,
And then
I have tears
On my face.
They roll
Out of my eyes,
Down onto my cheeks,
And off of my chin.
Sometimes,
My mommy
Takes one of my tears
On her finger,
And kisses it,
And puts it
Onto her face.
My mommy loves me.
When I am
Hurt or very sad,
My mommy is
Hurt or very sad, too.

October 1993

9

Reality

Sometimes,
I really miss
Having a brother.
I miss my
Two brothers and my sister,
And I don't
Understand
Why they died.
Sometimes,
It's so sad
To not have
A brother, and
Another brother, and
A sister
When I should have them.
And I know that
Something
Will make me
Happy again.
But, right now,
I don't know what, and
I don't know when.

January 1995

Little Boy Blue

Sometimes,
I am very, very, very sad.
And I don't know why.
But I know I am
Alone with my tears.
I am not angry,
But I am so sad.
I miss Jamie.
I want him to come back,
So I can touch him again.
Sometimes,
My mommy and my Mr. Bunny
Touch my tears.
They hold me and rock me,
And love my tears away,
Out of my eyes,
And off of my cheeks.
I am still sad then,
And I still miss Jamie,
But sometimes,
I am a little bit happier.

November 1993

At Mommy's Work

Today I went to my mommy's work with her.
I played with my work-friends,
Emily and Andrew.
Their mommies work, too.
We ate in a restaurant,
And I let my lunch balloon
Go up to the sky
And into Heaven for my brother, Jamie.
I ran and ran with my work-friends,
And then my heart hurt
Next to my belly-button
And I asked Mommy
To put on my oxygen-wind.
I was sad and tired and hurt.
But then the little boy work-friend
Covered his head with rubberbands.
He covered his ears and his nose, too,
He covered the floor and even the hall.
It was so silly of him.
And I laughed and laughed and laughed.
I was not sad anymore.
Then his mommy told him to clean up,
And he was not silly anymore,
So I did not laugh anymore.
But in the car going home,
I fell asleep,
And when I woke up,
I remembered my silly work-friend,
And I laughed and laughed
And laughed again.

December 1993

13

a-byss´

My life
Is halfway down
An abyss.
A deep
Immeasurable space.
A gulf.
A cavity.
A vast chasm.
My life
Is not how
I planned it to be.
Is not how
I want it to be.
Is not how
I pray for it
To be.
In the darkness
Of this pit,
I see a small
Light of hope.

Is it possible for me
To climb to such heights?
To rebuild the bridges?
To find my salvation?
The song
In my heart
Is so quiet.
Is so dark.
Is so fearful.
I dare not stay in
This abyss.
Though deep
And vast,
I am only halfway
Down.
Thus, I am
Already
Halfway up?
Let such words
Fall onto my heart,
And raise me from this depth.

January 2001

14

Bravery Prayer

Dear God,
Help us to always be able
To use the feelings of
Hope and fear, together,
In one great force...
Bravery.
Bravery is extremely
Necessary in life.
If we are able
To have bravery,
We will be able
To achieve
Many goals in life.
Amen.

December 1999

15

Life: That's Amazing!

When it is nighttime,
I get my nebulizer and All my medicines,
I go to the bathroom and brush my teeth,
I put on my pajamas and heart monitor,
And untangle my oxygen-mustache
So I get my special breathing wind.
When I am in my bed,
My mommy will read me a book,
And say my prayers with me.
She will kiss me and hug me and tuck me in,
And then turn on my Mommy-Songs tape.
When I close my eyes,
I go to sleep and dream and dream,
Or I go to sleep and do not dream.
When it is morning,
I wake up.
I am alive, and
I am breathing, and
I am a real boy.
That's Amazing!

October 1993

Morning Alarm

When I wake up
In the morning
After a night
When I have
A lot of alarms
For not breathing and
For low heart rate,
I forget so many things.
I cannot concentrate.
I am impatient.
And even though
It all gets better as
The day goes on,
I feel like I have
Young person's
Al Simer's disease.

April 2000

Beyond the Pain

I am looking out of the window.
I see so many beautiful things.
I see trucks and cars,
And flowers and plants,
And people.
I like looking out of the window.
People are such beautiful things.

September 1993

Hope
for
Each Other

19

Fair Feelings

Everyone has feelings—
Love, fear, sadness,
Happiness, confusion, hope…
Feelings depend on one's
Personal situation at a given time.
We should feel free and
Encouraged to express feelings,
But never in a way
That hurts the feelings of others.
Even if a person does not think
It is a big deal to say something
That could upset another person,
It could be a very crushing
Experience to that person.
It could affect the rest
Of his or her life, and
Possibly, even the lives of others
Subsequently touched by that person.
Attitudes are contagious.

March 2000

About Feelings

Some things hurt my feelings.
Like when other people tease me.
I have been teased by kids
About my oxygen, and
About not being able to keep up.
I have been teased by kids
For not teasing other kids,
And for setting a moral example.
I have been teased by someone
For not keeping scary secrets, and
For being afraid of threatening things.
I have even been teased by someone
About having a disability.
When things have hurt my feelings,
Usually I try to talk
To the person who has hurt me.
Sometimes, I have to talk
To a person I trust instead.
It is important for people to be
Honest when expressing themselves.
But, it is also important to be
Always thoughtful and considerate
In expressing feelings to others,
So that more feelings are not hurt.

March 2000

On Saying "Good-bye"

There are too many
Good-byes in my life.
Just too many,
Too many,
Too many good-byes.
Things were so sad,
And then,
Things were so bad,
And now,
Things are so much better,
But, I have to say
"Good-bye"—
And even though there
Will be another "hello,"
I don't want to see the
Friends and times of this
Best-of-all-summers go.
And if only my friends
Could be with me a
Little longer,
Just one more week—
I'd have seven more
Whole days
Before I'd have to cry.

July 1998

Lunch Hour

This was really not a very good day.
I played with my friend, Lissa,
And we began to argue
And hit at each other.
At first, I thought it felt good
  because
That's what Lissa does with her
  sister.
When they argue, they hit at each
  other.
So when I hit at Lissa,
I thought maybe it would be
Just like if my sister, Katie,
Was still alive and we were
  arguing.
But it didn't really feel good.
And when I told Mommy about it,
She was disappointed that I hit.
She said we touch gently in our
  family.
She said if Katie was alive,
We would probably argue,
But hitting would not be okay.

Mommy told me to sit and think
About how to disagree, but not
  hurt.
Then I knew it was not a very
  good day.
I tried to think about why I hit
  Lissa.
I don't want to be mean.
I don't always have to get my way.
I don't think I am a bad boy.
So I think that perhaps I hit Lissa
Because God went out to lunch,
And he could not come into my
  heart
And remind me to be peaceful
  when I was angry.
I sure hope God doesn't go out
  often.

January 1996

Examination of Faith (II)

Dear God,
When Mommy told me that
The little baby growing in Margie
Died last night,
I was surprised and angry.
I prayed to You, God.
I prayed every night and
I prayed every day and
We all prayed that this
Sweet little baby would live.
When Mommy told me that
The baby died, I said,
"Then our prayers didn't work!
God didn't listen! God didn't
Make a miracle for the baby!"
Mommy said that You
Always listen to our prayers,
But sometimes Your answer
Is not what we were wishing for,

And "prayers" are not "wishes."
She said that maybe letting
The baby come into Heaven
As such a tiny angel was a
  miracle.
There are miracles every single day
Except we don't always notice them,
Because we were hoping or
  wanting for
Something different than what
  we got.
So God,
Thank You for all the miracles
You give to us each day,
And thank You for listening
To *all* of our prayers.
And even though I am sad about
Margie's baby, I am not angry
  with You.
Amen.

March 1996

25

Possession

One of my greatest fears is "It."
I cannot touch It, but I can feel It,
And I can sense It with me.
It does not have a smell or taste,
But I can hear It in my trepidating
  spirit.
It has been bothering me
Since my home was broken
Into many times,
And I believe that the root
Of my fears are related
To great fears of a memory.
My fear of It causes me
To touch things again
And again and again
With certain parts of my hands,
Or to check door locks
And light switches again
And again and again.
It seems to control me at times,
But I am working to control It,

By running away, by ignoring It,
By directing my mind to some-
  thing else,
Or sometimes, by standing up to It
Regardless of how plutonic
The situation may be.
Although my mind has been
  threatened
Such that my life revolves around
  my fears,
I am learning to understand
That It can never possess me.
See, in grammar, the word "it"
Can never be possessive;
It can never be contracted into
  ownership.
And so, now that I understand this,
I am trying so hard to believe
That the concept of It
Will never get me, possess me,
  hurt me.
One day, I may finally defeat It.
Then, I can at last live my life
Fearlessly, peacefully, hopefully,
And with gentle happiness.

February 2000

About Confidence

Trying new things
Is important.
And, we must believe
In ourselves,
And have confidence
To achieve a goal.
If we don't believe
We can complete a task,
Doubt will take over,
And we may slowly
Back away from the task,
Until we have altogether
Quit working towards the goal.
So, every day,
We must have confidence
In what we are doing.

When we believe in ourselves,
Our spirits become more open
To new things
That are good and healthy.
It also closes up more
To bad and unhealthy
Things in life.
Trying new things
Is important.
And, if we believe
In ourselves,
And have confidence,
We can achieve
So many exciting goals.

May 2000

It's Okay, Little Prince

It's okay, Little Prince,
I want to go home, too.
I can see it in your eyes,
I can hear it in your cries,
Can you see it in me, too?
It's okay, Little Prince,
I want to be home, too.
I can sense it in your mind,
I can feel it in your heart-so-kind,
Can you sense it in me, too?
It's okay, Little Prince,
I want to feel home, too.
But for now, I'll help you cope,
And for now, I'll give you hope,
Will you help me out, too?

July 2001

About Dreamland

There is a place called Dreamland.
It is where you travel about
When you first rest into sleep.
You dream that you are in clouds
With ladders and stairs that lead you
Until you get to Dreamland's castle.
In the castle, there are pictures,
Lots of pictures,
And the pictures are good dreams.
Watch your step, though,
Or you might get sucked into the ground.
And in the ground are bad dreams.
In the good dream pictures,
You still watch your steps carefully,
Because the dreams are all the ones
Of your life, and also some more.
They are all of what was or almost was,
And what might be even if it's good or bad.
You can choose any one of the pictures
That you want, so relax and take your time.
Look around and you will see that
There are millions and millions and
More people there, finding dreams and
Jumping into the pictures to their thoughts.
And now, I will leave you tonight, and everynight,
In the Kingdom of Dreamland.
Jump into the good dreams,
But step carefully watching for the bad dreams.
Sleep well, and good night.

September 1997

32

Rolter's Wisdom

You may be tall,
I may be small,
But inside...
We are the same
Length of strength

June 1998

Both Sides

Every privilege
Comes with
A responsibility.
Sounds tough.
Every responsibility
Comes with a privilege.
Sounds durable.

November 2000

Thought S'pan

Everyone has a happy thought that
Inspires them to fly into their future...
My happy thought begins with
My mother, who came before me.
My happy thought continues with
My brothers and sister, who are with me.
My happy thought proceeds with
My children, who will come from me.
Everyone has a happy thought that
Inspires them to fly into their future...
My happy thought is kinship.

May 2000

Songs of the Wind

Listen to the wind.
If you listen carefully,
You will hear soft notes.
Listen with your mind and
Heart—you will hear a song.
A soft, relaxing song that
Reminds you of peace,
Harmony, and love.
If you hear this song,
Always remember it.
For if you do,
You can teach it
To other people,
And they, too, will forever
Remember their Heartsongs.

July 1998

When the Trees Sing

When the trees sing,
It doesn't really matter
If you know the song,
Or if you know the words,
Or even if you know the tune.
What really matters is knowing
That the trees are singing at all.

May 1998

Hope for Life's Journey

Someday,
I'd like to see what's down every road.
I'd like to travel across
Every highway and every byway.
I'd like to explore
Every mountain pass and every sandy trail.
I'd like to follow
Every straight route and every winding path.
Someday,
I'd like to understand
From where all things come,
And to what all things are destined.
Someday,
Even though I am sure of my lesson—
That we are all hoping to the same place—
I'd like to take the time
To travel and explore and follow,
So that I can really see and understand
What's down every road.

August 2001

36

Hope
for
Our World

About Perseverance

No matter how hard
People strive for peace,
We are not all unified
In the goal, and so,
It is always out of reach
For the world as a whole.
But, it does not, and should not,
Have to be that way.
If we all help each other,
And work together
Day after night after day,
We can achieve a great goal:
World harmony and peace,
For you and me and us.

August 2000

39

Only One

Only one murder should have been done.
Only one bomb should have been blown.
Oh please, there should have been
Only one hurt to cry out to the Lord.
More than one murder,
More than one bomb,
More than one hurt,
Does not make it right,
Even if saying, "They started the fight!"
Only one of these things was
More than enough.
Only one.
Only one.
But not only one
Can make peace in the world.

February 1998

Just Peace

If I could change
One thing in this world,
It would be war.
Instead of war…peace.
But I especially don't want
World War Three,
Because we would
Blow up the earth.
If I could change
One thing in this world
We would have no weapons.
No knives or swords.
No guns or bombs.
Just peace.
Just peace.

February 1998

So What If...

What If the world fills up
With so many people,
That the earth can't hold us all?
Is that a reason for war?
No.
Is that a reason not to love unborn babies?
No.
Is that a reason to let sick people die?
No.
It is a reason we need to make extra room,
First in our hearts, and
Then into our world.
It is a reason to make room for prayer,
Because God is the only "I AM"
Who can answer such a "What If."

February 1998

Salvation

The world must
Never waste
A memory,
No matter
How it
Makes one feel.
For every
Memory is a
Gift of God.
And, every
Gift of God
That the world uses
Is another step
Towards
Each-otherness,
And peace.

June 2000

43

In a Mountain Storm Cloud

We were up in
The mountains,
High in the sky.
It was raining.
But we were not
As wet.
For we were in the
Mountain storm cloud,
Understanding the rain
As it went down, down
Below the valley.
We were up in
The Heavens,
Watering the earth below,
Washing away the sadness
That grows from
Anger and fear.

August 1998

The Bigger Picture

Mommy said we should pray
For the little children
And the grown-ups who died
When the mean and nasty
Men put a bomb in the building
In Oklahoma.
I will pray for them,
But they are all in Heaven.
We are sad,
But they are happy.
I think who we really
Need to pray for
Are the men who
Did such a sad thing.
They are the ones who
Do not have God in their hearts.
They are the ones who
Will not go to Heaven
When they die.
So I think we should
Pray for them, too,
So that maybe
They will learn to be sorry
For what they did,
And learn to be good people.

April 1995

When Warnings Are Ignored

Right now,
The whole world is "Mr. Yuk."
The little children know to stay away
When they see the stickers and
   the signs.
The big people don't see them though,
But that's because they close
Their own eyes...you know.
They don't want to see the
Warnings and poisons of war.
How it kills our children,
Our people, our earth.
They have "reasons" for fighting
Anyplace, Anywhere.
They have "reasons" for killing in
Bosnia, Iraq, and Zaire.
They fight about God
And how people pray.
They fight about fighting...

They just fight and fight
And fight, Everyday.
There is anger in families
And even in schools.
People don't want to follow
The laws and the rules...
Unless they made them or like them.
But that is not right.
That just isn't right.
That thinking just poisons
Respect and responsibility
   and life.
Poisoned thoughts
Turn into poisoned actions,
Which causes the war and fight.
And so,
Even though we should see
The warning signs Everywhere,
We don't look with our hearts,
And the whole world is "Mr. Yuk."

March 1998

46

Past, Present, Future

Shrouded in white,
Dark ninja knight.
Hooded, each man,
Dreadful east Klan.
Masked to be super,
Wicked storm trooper.
Marching in rows,
Planning low blows.
No soul to claim,
Unspeakable name.
Evil of hatin'...
Army of Satan.

February 2001

Attack on America

A wild bomb will consume
Morning, evening, and all people,
Showering dirt to burn man's skin.

September 11, 2001

47

9-11...2001

It was a dark day in America.
There was no amazing grace.
Freedom did not ring.
Tragedy attacked sky-high.
Fiery terror reigned.
Structures collapsed.
Red with blood, white with ash,
And out-of-the-sky blue.
As children trust elders,
Citizens find faith in leaders.
But all were blinded,
Shocked by the blasts.
Undefiable outrage.
Undeniable outpouring
Of support, even prayer,
Or at least, moments of silence.
Church and State
Could not be separated.
A horrific blasting of events
With too few happy endings.
Can the children sleep
Safely in their beds tonight?
Can the citizens ever rest
Assured of national security again?
God, please, bless America...
And the rest of our earthly home.

September 11, 2001

For Our World

We need to stop.
Just stop.
Stop for a moment...
Before anybody
Says or does anything
That may hurt anyone else.
We need to be silent.
Just silent.
Silent for a moment...
Before we forever lose
The blessing of songs
That grow in our hearts.
We need to notice.
Just notice.
Notice for a moment...
Before the future slips away
Into ashes and dust of humility.

Stop, be silent, and notice...
In so many ways, we are the same.
Our differences are unique treasures.
We have, we are, a mosaic of gifts
To nurture, to offer, to accept.
We need to be.
Just be.
Be for a moment...
Kind and gentle, innocent and
    trusting,
Like children and lambs,
Never judging or vengeful
Like the judging and vengeful.
And now, let us pray,
Differently, yet together,
Before there is no earth, no life,
No chance for peace.

September 2001

49

Peace

The sun feels warm on our bodies and hands.
But, if we touch the sun, it would burn.
It makes things bright and beautiful,
But, if we look at it, it hurts our eyes.
The sun doesn't make any noise,
And we can't taste it, or smell it.
I guess that's why the sun stays
So far away from us.
The sun is our friend,
But we can't do anything with it,
And we can't touch it or look at it,
Except when it first comes in the morning,
Or when it is leaving in the evening.
Then we can look at the
Sunrise and the sunset,
And see how wonderful
Our friend the sun is.
But we still can't touch it,
Because it would hurt, and
Friends don't hurt friends.

October 1993

50

Morning Gift

Don't you love the mornings
When you go outside,
And there on the ground
Is a fresh, perfect, green leaf?
A leaf, floated from the
Quiet summer trees,
Just resting on the grass, and
Waiting to be discovered.
Touch the treasure, and
Pick it up gently, then
Feel all the excitement of
A new leaf, with no tears,
No marks, no holes.
It is a sign of healing and future.
Don't you just love the mornings
When you are reminded of
The special gifts of life?

June 1999

52

Revolutions 365.25

When the moon sets
Over your shoulder
As the sun rises
Bright towards your face,
What's in the middle?
Your life is...
Filled with choices
For each moment, each place.
We live between the
Past and the future,
In the moment of our
Here, now, today.
Can we cope with the
Daily life stresses?
If we humbly accept...
We must pray.

December 2001

53

Life Is Like...

Life is like a story book...
Although we aren't
Able to talk with
Dragons and fly far into space,
Each day is like
A new chapter,
With new lessons
For our lives.
Life is like a dream...
Although we don't
Know what kind of
Reverie we will have,
Each day is like
A new thought,
With new hopes
For our lives.
Life is like a great waiting...
Although we can't
Realize when or how,
Each day is like
A new chance,
With new opportunities
For our lives.

As we travel and learn
And think and hope
And chance opportunities
In each day of our lives,
We must understand
That anytime
Could be the Time
That we face the fact of Heaven,
And never have to fear again.
So each day,
We should live out
The great dream and story
That our lives are waiting to be...
For we know
And we are able
And we realize that
Life is like
Whatever we create it to be.

August 2000

54

Future Reminiscing

It is good
To have a past
That is pleasant
To reflect upon.
Take care
To create
Such a gift
For your future.

December 2000

The Way Home

Sometimes the way home is love.
Sometimes the way home is together.
And sometimes the way home is
Not just love,
But loving each other.
And sometimes the way home is
Not just together,
But together with other people...
  People you love a lot,
  People you like a lot, and
  People you are friends with.
But all of the times, the way home is
Every good thing that God told us to do.

January 1996

Momentous Reality

The next century, the next millennium
Is being made, now, Today, each
  second.
We could be working towards
World peace, living as one spirit.
Or, we could be working towards
Disaster, chemical and nuclear
  wars.
The harmony, and existence of
  the future
Depends on the harmony and
  existence
Of each individual here, today.
We must be brave going into the
  future.
We must remember to play after
  each storm.
We must not live in fear of bad
  things
Blocking our way or overcoming
  our optimism.
If we can work together to face
  the future,
If we can unite as one,
Then our future will look, and be,
  very bright.

Even though the future seems far
  away,
It is actually beginning right now.
And while we are living in the
  present,
We must celebrate life everyday,
Knowing that we are becoming
  history
With every word, every action, every
  moment.
Because we, today, are the history
  of tomorrow,
We must ask ourselves each day
What we are doing that may have
An influence on the future.
It really won't be for many years that
The future will indicate if something
  we said,
Or if something we did or did not do,
Had an impact on a single individual,
Or if it trickled out to touch the
  whole world.

February 2000

Faith Imagery

I can imagine non-existence.
Can you?
It's not like being dead,
But it's not being alive.
There is no light,
But the dark is nothingness.
It is not painful,
But it feels horrible.
It is being stuck
Between not having been,
And having been but being gone.
There is no feeling in non-existence,
But it is the most alone thing
Of loneliness one could imagine.
I can imagine non-existence.
I thank God everyday,
For the gift of faith...
For it is in faith,
That I will exist, forever.
I can imagine non-existence,
And I hope and pray
That you can, too,
For Ever.

October 1999

Believing in Someday

Maybe,
Someday,
We will all join hands
And live together...
Helping each other,
Loving each other.
Maybe,
Someday,
We will all make the world
A much better place...
And be like a gigantic,
Smoothly rushing river of peace—
A loving circle that nothing can break.
Maybe,
Someday,
We may start with just one person,
And one permanent peace agreement
Within one's self, within one's world.

Personal peace can then spread
Within and between the families,
Then within and between communities,
And then within and around the
  whole world.
Maybe,
Someday,
We can become
As close to perfect
As anything and anyone can get.
Let us each join our own Heartsong
With this old song of the heart, and
  believe...
  "Let there be peace on earth,
  And let it begin with me."

August 2000

Facing the Future

Every journey begins
With but a small step.
And every day is a chance
For a new, small step
In the right direction.
Just follow your Heartsong.

December 1998

Index

7-24-09   BB NT